LEADER'S GUIDE

NAVPRESS

A MINISTRY OF THE NAVIGATORS
P.O. BOX 35001, COLORADO SPRINGS, COLORADO 80935

This *Leader's Guide* is designed for use with the 1980 revised edition of *Design for Discipleship* in which a different system for numbering questions is introduced. But it is also easily adaptable for use with the previous edition. Just follow these instructions: Rather than using the numbers in this guide which are listed next to the headings and discussion questions, use the section headings themselves (the headings in bold type) to help you match the discussion questions here with the appropriate section in each chapter of the study books. In this way you can fully discuss each chapter section by section.

For comprehensive help in organizing, leading, and evaluating Bible study discussion groups, read *How to Lead Small Groups* by Neal McBride (NavPress, 1990).

The Navigators is an international Christian organization. Jesus Christ gave His followers the Great Commission to go and make disciples (Matthew 28:19). The aim of The Navigators is to help fulfill that commission by multiplying laborers for Christ in every nation.

NavPress is the publishing ministry of The Navigators. NavPress publications are tools to help Christians grow. Although publications alone cannot make disciples or change lives, they can help believers learn biblical discipleship, and apply what they learn to their lives and ministries.

© 1980 by The Navigators
All rights reserved. No part of this publication may be reproduced in any form without written permission from NavPress, P.O. Box 35001, Colorado Springs, CO 80935.
ISBN 08910-90436

Seventeenth printing, 1993

Printed in the United States of America

FOR A FREE CATALOG OF
NAVPRESS BOOKS & BIBLE STUDIES,
CALL 1-800-366-7788 (USA)
or 1-416-499-4615 (CANADA)

The Bible is a written record of God's love for us. He has given it for our good. From the Scriptures we can begin to know what he is like, what he has done for us, and what he asks us to do.

But the Navigator Bible study series *Design for Discipleship* is more than a tool for helping someone grow in knowledge of the Scriptures. And your goal as a group leader should be higher than that too.

Design for Discipleship is a tool for *developing disciples of Jesus Christ*. Knowing more of the Bible is only part of this. Far more important is actually putting into practice what has been learned from the Bible. Don't settle for a lesser aim in your group. Reach high.

Of course the seven *Design for Discipleship* books are only tools. God does the actual work of raising up a disciple. But through a combination of factors—your group's openness to learn, your prayer for them, and your own example and leadership—these books can be instruments in the hand of God's Spirit to transform their lives—and yours.

Who should be in the group?
Design for Discipleship is a comprehensive study on the basic biblical principles and standards for following Jesus Christ. It is for everyone who desires to be his disciple. The series can be used by high school students, collegians, or adults. It is for married couples or singles, men or women.

Those who are considering a *Design for Discipleship* Bible study should be aware from the beginning that study preparation for each group discussion is necessary. You may want to

3

show them Book One and page through one of the chapters to let them see how much weekly preparation is involved.

This series is appropriate for Sunday school classes and for smaller and less formal groups, such as home Bible studies, "growth" groups, and Christian businessmen's meetings.

Usually a group size of from six to ten is the most conducive to good discussion. If your group is larger, consider dividing into smaller groups.

Your schedule
Altogether, the seven *Design for Discipleship* books have 36 chapters. A good pace is to study and discuss one chapter per week. All seven books could be completed this way in nine months (three quarters).

Your total discussion time each week should probably not exceed one hour. Start and end on time.

Your first meeting
When your group meets for the first time you will probably find it best to accomplish these three things:
- Establish a relaxed atmosphere, making sure everyone is acquainted and at ease with you and with each other.
- Tell them what they need to know about the *Design for Discipleship* books and about how your group will operate.
- Make sure everyone knows what to study in preparation for your next meeting.

To establish a relaxed atmosphere in a group of people who may not know each other well, spend a few minutes having each person give information about himself such as his name, his home city, where he lives now, and his occupation. If you give this information first it will set the others more at ease, letting them know how much to say.

You can also tell what has drawn each of you to God and made you want to study the Bible. Again, you should take the lead in telling this.

Make sure each group member has a Bible and a copy of *Design for Discipleship* Book One. (If you haven't already, you may want to ask them now to faithfully prepare each chapter and attend each discussion for Book One, after which they can reevaluate their commitment to the group.)

Have everyone turn in Book One to the introduction on page 3. Ask various group members to each read a paragraph aloud until you have read together the entire page. Then ask if

4

they have any questions. You may want to explain in your own words that Book One is about God and his care for us, Jesus Christ and his death and resurrection, and the Holy Spirit's presence in us.

Then turn to page 5 and have someone read the opening paragraphs in Chapter 1. To help the group become familiar with the kind of preparation they will be doing on their own each week, answer together some of the questions in this first chapter. You may want to do three or four questions at the beginning, or select a few from other parts of the chapter.

Your aim in this is simply to make them feel at ease about how to complete their study. Have one person read the question aloud, and then have everyone look up the related Scripture reference. (You may need to have copies of the Bible available for them if some did not bring one.) Then have someone else read aloud the Scripture passage. You may want to read it from various translations. Talk together about how you would answer the question, and then have each person write the answer in his book.

Briefly look over pages 5-10 to see how long Chapter 1 is, and tell the group that this is the material they should complete by your next meeting. Confirm the time and place for that meeting.

Leading the discussions
As the leader, take charge in an inoffensive way. The group is looking to you for good leadership.

You may want to experiment with various methods for discussing the study material. One simple approach is to discuss it question by question. You can do this by going around the group in order, with the first person giving his answer to question one (followed by discussion), the second person answering question two, and so on.

This method can be a good way to introduce Bible study discussion to those who have never been a part of a Bible study group. The obvious structure gives them a sense of confidence, and they can easily follow the direction of the discussion.

Another discussion method is the section-by-section approach. This can provide more spontaneity. Point out to the group that each chapter in Book One is divided into sections. In Chapter 1 these sections are "God Created You," "God Knows You," "God Loves You," and "God Made You Part of His Family."

Start the discussion by asking the group for its impressions of the first section. Say something like, "What impressed you most from this section called 'God Created You'?" Remember to direct your question to the entire group, rather than to a certain person.

Someone will probably give an answer by referring to a specific question in that section. You can have others share their answers to the same question. Then, to discuss the answers more thoroughly, ask one or two thought-provoking questions which you have prepared beforehand.

For example, someone in the group may say that the most impressive thing in the section "God Created You" is what he learned from Genesis 1 in question five, that man is created in God's image. A few others may want to comment on this, and then you could ask, "What evidence can we see today that every person is created in God's image?"

You can then ask others what things most impressed them from this first section. After talking about these and asking questions to stimulate further discussion, go on to the next section.

Preparing for each discussion

Two keys to a more interesting and helpful discussion are having an overall objective for each chapter, and having good discussion questions prepared.

This leader's guide includes information that can help you prepare in these two areas. A suggested chapter objective is listed for each chapter in all seven *Design for Discipleship* books. Following the objective are sample discussion questions. You will also find blank lines to write your own discussion questions.

> Also included are guidelines to help you improve your leadership skills each week. These are enclosed in boxes like this.

BOOK ONE

YOUR LIFE IN CHRIST

CHAPTER ONE
GOD CARES FOR YOU

Chapter objective: *To see that we can be assured of our salvation in Christ—an assurance based on scriptural evidence.*

Remember that your group members have put time and effort into answering the questions in their study book. Many will be eager to share with the group what they have discovered. The focus of your discussion should be on what has impressed them from their own study.

You will want to have several discussion questions prepared to help stimulate the group to talk freely about what they have learned. A few suggestions are listed below for each section of Chapter 1. Use the blank lines to write your own discussion questions.

These questions from the chapter may promote the best discussion in your group: 5, 10, 12, 14, and 16.

At the end of this and all the other chapters you may want to have different group members read aloud the various statements listed under the heading "Remember These Points."

You may also want someone to read aloud the three assurance verses on page 9.

God Created You (Questions 1-5)
4 Why is it important to realize that God created us?
5 Why is man unique?
5 What things in our lives do not reflect God-likeness?

Use these blank lines to write your own discussion questions:

_____

_____

_____

_____

_____

God Knows You (6-8)
6-8 In what ways is it important to know that God fully knows us?

6-8 How can we benefit from God's complete knowledge of us?

6 How do we try to hide things from God?

_____

_____

_____

_____

_____

God Loves You (9-12)

9 Why do you think God loves us?

10 What was God's overall purpose in sending Christ? 🖎

_____

_____

_____

_____

_____

God Made You Part of His Family (13-16)

13-16 What are our responsibilities as members of God's family?

16 What does it mean that we are "heirs of God and co-heirs with Christ?"

_____

_____

_____

_____

_____

Summary

Complete this statement: I know God loves me because . . . .

It is often good at the beginning of the discussion to provide a broad overview of the chapter. Cover the key ideas and how they relate to each other.

CHAPTER TWO
THE PERSON OF JESUS CHRIST

Chapter objective: *To see how Jesus Christ is both God and man, and that therefore he is the sole mediator between God and man.*

Good questions for discussion are 9, 10, 11, and 15.
You may want to have someone read aloud the introductory paragraphs at the beginning of this chapter.
Before you pray together to close the meeting, you could have each person share a current prayer request.

The Deity of Jesus Christ (Questions 1-10)
1-10 What did Christ show the world about God?
1-10 How did Jesus demonstrate that he was God?
  2 Since Jesus was born 2,000 years ago, how could he be the Creator?
6-8 Could Jesus' work have been done by any human? Explain your answer.
  7 What is important to you about the resurrection of Lazarus?
 10 How is Christ's authority affecting your life today?

_____

_____

_____

_____

_____

The Humanity of Jesus Christ (11-15)
11-15 What human characteristics did Jesus exhibit?
 12 What is temptation?
 15 Why was it necessary for God to become human?
 15 How does Christ's humanity help us relate to God?

_____

_____

_____

_____

_____

Summary

How do you know Jesus is God?

How do you know Jesus is human?

If your group members take away one or two things from their Bible study preparation and discussion that they begin to apply in their lives, success has been achieved.

CHAPTER THREE
THE WORK OF CHRIST

Chapter objective: *To gain a better understanding of the elements of the gospel—that Christ died for our sins, and was resurrected from the dead for our sake.*

Good questions for discussion are 5, 8, 11, and 16. You may want to have someone read aloud Edward Clarke's quote on page 22.

The Life of Jesus Christ (Questions 1-5)
1-5 What one aspect of Jesus' life impresses you most?
1-5 How was Jesus' life like that of any other man?
1-5 How was his life different from other men's?
3 What is "the gospel of the kingdom"?
4 Why did Jesus want the disciples to be with him?

_____

_____

_____

_____

The Death of Jesus Christ (6-11)
6-11 What reasons can you list for Jesus' death?
7 Why was Jesus crucified instead of being killed by some other means?
9 Why can't God ignore our sin?
6-11 How are God's demands met by Christ's death?

_____

_____

_____

_____

The Resurrection of Jesus Christ (12-16)
12-16 Would Jesus' death have any meaning without his resurrection? Explain your answer.
14 Why did the Jews bribe the guards?

12

15 When the disciples first saw Jesus, why did they react as they did?

16 Can a person be a Christian and not believe in Christ's resurrection?

16 Why is there power in the resurrection message?

_____

_____

_____

_____

_____

Summary

If God could do it over again, do you think he would permit Jesus to die?

Be sure to have clearly in mind the goal for each chapter as you prepare for and lead the chapter discussion. There must be a goal for your time. It is your responsibility to keep this goal in focus.

CHAPTER FOUR
THE SPIRIT WITHIN YOU

Chapter objective: *To understand that the Holy Spirit lives in all who believe in Christ, and enables us to obey Christ.*

Good questions for discussion are 6, 10, 12, and 20.

At the end of this session, point out to the group that the Wheel Illustration on page 29 in their study books serves as the outline for their study in Book Two. The five chapters in Book Two cover the five topics of obedience, God's word, prayer, fellowship, and witnessing. You may want to have the group memorize this illustration and be able to draw it at your next meeting.

Jesus Christ's Ascension (Questions 1-3)

1 How will Jesus come again?
2 What do you think it means that Jesus is preparing a place for us?

_____

_____

_____

_____

_____

_____

Jesus Christ's Work of Intercession (4-6)

5 What impressed you most from this prayer of Jesus?

_____

_____

_____

_____

_____

The Indwelling Holy Spirit (7-12)

9 Why must we have God's Spirit to understand what God has given us (1 Corinthians 2:12)?
12 How can a person know that he has the Holy Spirit?

_____

_____

_____

_____

_____

Living Under the Holy Spirit's Control (13-20)
13-20 Why do we need the Holy Spirit in our lives?
   13 What is the difference between being controlled by
       the Holy Spirit and being indwelt by the Holy
       Spirit?
13-20 What is the Holy Spirit doing today in your life?

_____

_____

_____

_____

_____

Summary
Complete this sentence: I know the Holy Spirit lives
within me because . . . .

> If you show that you recognize the worth of every per-
> son in the group, the others will follow your example
> and will also respect and appreciate each other.

EVALUATING YOUR LEADERSHIP

You can use these self-evaluation questions following each session to help you improve your leadership in the future:
1. Did you know the material well enough to have freedom in leading?
2. Did you have enough questions prepared to properly guide the discussion?
3. Did you discuss the major points in the chapter?
4. Was the discussion practical?
5. Did you keep the discussion from wandering?
6. Did everyone participate?
7. Did you begin and end on time?

BOOK TWO

THE SPIRIT-FILLED CHRISTIAN

CHAPTER ONE
THE OBEDIENT CHRISTIAN

Chapter objective: *To see that obedience is the most important quality of our love for Jesus Christ.*

You may want to begin this session by reviewing the Wheel Illustration—a key tool for helping us evaluate how balanced our Christian life is.

Have someone read aloud the introduction to Book Two on page 3.

Good questions for discussion are 4, 14, 15, 18, and 21.

The Basis for Obedience (Questions 1-4)
1 How does our understanding of who God is in-fluence our obedience to him?
2 Why is it for our good to obey God?
4 How important is love in our relationship with God?

_____

_____

_____

_____

_____

_____

Obedience to God (5-8)
5-8 Why is the Bible crucial in the matter of obedience?

_____

_____

_____

_____

_____

Keys to Consistent Obedience (9-12)
9-12 Describe God's part and your part in your living an obedient life.
12 Why are our attitudes important in obedience?

_____

_____

_____

_____

_____

The Practice of Obedient Living (13-21)

13 What is the difference between temptation and sin?

15 Do people fall into sin or plan for it?

16-17 What is God's remedy for sin?

17 Since God knows everything, why should we confess our sins?

19 In what areas of your life have you had victory over sin lately?

_____

_____

_____

_____

_____

Summary

How do you know you can have victory over sin?

How do you know God forgives you when you sin?

Remember to pray faithfully and regularly for your group members. Each one will have distinct needs you can pray about. Learn what these are.

19

CHAPTER TWO
GOD'S WORD IN YOUR LIFE

Chapter objective: *To become convinced of the importance of the Scriptures as God's personal communication to us; to decide to spend time each day in reading the Scriptures.*

Encourage your group members to begin memorizing Bible passages through The Navigators' *Topical Memory System.* You could have the group review their most recently memorized verses at the beginning of each discussion session. Tell them how important Scripture memory is to you.

Be sure to discuss the Hand Illustration on page 19, and have the group memorize this before your next session.

Good discussion questions are 4, 11, and 13.

God's Word—His Communication to You (Questions 1-4)

    1   How do you know the Bible is God's word?
    3   Is truth absolute or relative? Why?
    4   How does the Bible spiritually refresh you?
    1-4 How does the Bible reflect God's character?

_____

_____

_____

_____

_____

How the Bible Helps You (5-6)

    5   How can the Bible be relevant today?
    6   How is the Bible like fire and a hammer (Jeremiah 23:29)?
    6   How is the Bible like bread (Matthew 4:4)?
    6   How is the Bible like a mirror? (James 1:23-25)?
    5-6 How has the Bible helped you recently?

_____

_____

_____

_____

_____

Your Responsibility (7-11)

7-11 How does God hold us responsible for knowing the Scriptures?

11 What does it mean to let the word of Christ dwell richly in us?

_____

_____

_____

_____

_____

The Importance of Meditation (12-13)

12-13 What is meditation?

12 How can we meditate on Scripture day and night?

13 How is a person's stability based on his relationship with God through the Scriptures?

_____

_____

_____

_____

_____

Summary

Why is absorbing and thinking about God's word important to you?

Your true goal in Bible study discussion should be helping your group members apply what they learn. Application should be something that can be measured in the immediate future.

CHAPTER THREE
CONVERSING WITH GOD

Chapter objective: *To see prayer as our God-given means of communication with him, and to decide to spend time each day in prayer.*

Good questions for discussion are 6, 8, 12, 13, and 16. At the end of the session, encourage your group members to begin using a prayer list. You may also want to give them a month-long quiet time plan (such as the one outlined in *Appointment with God* from NavPress) to help get them going in this vitally important discipline.

You could also suggest the booklet *My Heart Christ's Home* (InterVarsity Press) or the pamphlet *Seven Minutes with God* (NavPress) as additional reading.

Prayer—Your Communication with God (Questions 1-3)
1-3 What is necessary on our part to develop a relationship with God?
2 What does it mean to "pray continually" (1 Thessalonians 5:17)?

_____

_____

_____

_____

_____

The Benefits of Prayer (4-6)
4-6 How does God show that he is concerned about us?
4-6 What will be the results in our lives of meeting with God in prayer?

_____

_____

_____

_____

_____

_____

Conditions of Prayer (7-8)

    7 Why is faith essential when praying (Matthew 21:22)?

    7 What does it mean to ask in Jesus' name (John 16:24)?

    7-8 Should I pray if I don't meet the right conditions?

_____

_____

_____

_____

For Whom Do You Pray? (9-13)

    9-13 Have you found it helpful to use a prayer list?

_____

_____

_____

_____

_____

Daily Conversation with God (14-16)

    16 What is the main reason you spend time daily with God in Bible reading and prayer?

_____

_____

_____

_____

_____

Summary

Are you consistently meeting with God daily for time alone in prayer and Scripture reading and meditation? Why or why not?

Motivation is a key factor in learning. Help your group members see why learning the biblical view of discipleship is important.

CHAPTER FOUR
FELLOWSHIP WITH CHRISTIANS

Chapter objective: *To see that fellowship with other Christians is a biblical command, based on our need for each other.*

Good questions for discussion are 5, 9, and 19.

What Is Biblical Fellowship? (Questions 1-5)
1-5 When does fellowship take place?
  2 What are the most important things we can share with others?
  5 Are you satisfied with the level of fellowship you have with others?

_____

_____

_____

_____

_____

_____

The Purpose of Fellowship (6-9)
  6 Why is fellowship necessary for our personal growth?
  7 How do we stimulate each other to love?

_____

_____

_____

_____

_____

The Body of Christ (10-15)
  10 When it comes to fellowship, how can Christ be first in our lives?
  11 Why are all members necessary in the body of Christ?
10-15 Are you satisfied with the part you are playing in the body of Christ? If not, how can you change?

_____

_____

_____

_____

_____

The Local Church (16-20)
16-20 What are your responsibilities in the local church?

_____

_____

_____

_____

Summary
Why do you believe fellowship is important in your life?

In planning the discussion, it is often best to develop questions for the main study material first, and then plan how you will begin and end the discussion.

CHAPTER FIVE
WITNESSING FOR CHRIST

Chapter objective: *To see the importance of sharing with others what Jesus Christ has done for us, and to become more skilled in doing this.*

Allow plenty of time in this session for each group member to read aloud his personal testimony. You will want to find something to praise in each testimony, and perhaps mention one way in which it could be improved.

You may also want to give each group member a copy of the *Bridge to Life* evangelistic tract from NavPress, and explain how to use it in presenting the gospel.

Suggest LeRoy Eims' *Winning Ways* (Victor Books) or Lorne Sanny's *The Art of Personal Witnessing* (Moody Press) as outside reading.

Good questions for discussion are 2, 6, and 12.

The Challenge (Questions 1-5)
2 Why was Peter compelled to speak of Jesus?
5 How should seeking God's approval be a motive in our witnessing?

How Do You Become an Effective Witness? (6-12)
6-7 Why is love so important in witnessing?
8-9 What qualities of life make a person an effective witness?
10-12 How much do you need to know to speak to someone about your faith in Christ?

Paul's Story (13-17)
    14 What kind of man was Paul before he met Christ?
    15 How did Christ change Paul?
 13-17 What can you learn from Paul's story that is
         helpful to you?

_____

_____

_____

_____

_____

Your story
    Why is it important to write out your story of how you
    became a Christian?

Summary
    Why do you believe sharing your faith in Christ with
    others is important?

> Remember that discussion involves personal feelings
> as well as objective opinions about the subject matter.
> Don't make the mistake of being insensitive to these
> personal feelings.

HOW TO PRAY FOR YOUR GROUP

Your most important preparation for each session is prayer. You will want to make your requests personal, but here are some suggestions for praying each week:

- Pray that everyone in the group will complete the chapter preparation, and will attend this week's discussion. Ask God to help each of them to honestly share his thoughts, and to make a significant contribution to the discussion.
- Ask God to give each of them an understanding of what they study. Pray God will meet the unique needs of each person through this exposure to his word.
- Pray that as the leader you will know the Holy Spirit's guidance in exercising patience, acceptance, sensitivity, and wisdom. Pray for an atmosphere of genuine love in the group, with each member being honestly open to learning and change.
- Pray the result of your study and discussion will be that each person has greater confidence in the Bible and a willingness to obey the Lord by applying in his life the Scriptures you study.

BOOK THREE

WALKING WITH CHRIST

CHAPTER ONE
MATURING IN CHRIST

Chapter objective: *To recognize that spiritual growth is a long process that includes struggles.*

Encourage your group in Scripture memory, and allow time for reviewing recently learned verses.

Have someone read aloud the introduction to Book Three on page 3.

Good questions for discussion include 1, 6, 9, 10, and 20.

Moving toward Maturity (Questions 1-6)
1-6 How can you measure maturity?

  2 What is "unity in the faith" (Ephesians 4:13)?

  5 How does sanctification come about in our lives?

1-6 Are you more mature today than you were a year ago? How do you know?

_____

_____

_____

_____

_____

_____

Your Starting Point (7-9)
  7 What does it mean to be "rooted and built up" in Christ?

_____

_____

_____

_____

_____

The Process of Growth (10-14)
12 How does sin rule in one's life?

14 How have you seen God at work in your life recently?

_____

_____

_____

_____

_____

How to Live (15-16)
16 Which of these contrasts stand out to you as the most important?

_____

_____

_____

_____

The Mature Life (17-20)
19 How do we grow in grace (2 Peter 3:18)?

_____

_____

_____

_____

Summary
What do you think are the primary areas in which you are now growing spiritually?

Plan for social and recreational activities with your group outside your discussion sessions.

CHAPTER TWO
THE LORDSHIP OF CHRIST

Chapter objective: *To see that having Christ in control of our lives is the only way to have a fulfilling life, and to learn how to give him that control.*

Encourage your group to set personal goals in each area of the Wheel and Hand illustrations. Provide a pattern for them by developing and sharing with them your own goals. For example, in the area of prayer from the Wheel Illustration, your goal could be to pray through each item on your prayer list every day. In the area of memorization (from the Hand Illustration), your goal could be two memorized verses per week.

Good questions for discussion include 9, 10, 11, 13, and 19.

The Lord Jesus Christ (Questions 1-6)
1-6 What are some of the ways Jesus is Lord?

_____

_____

_____

_____

_____

Acknowledge His Lordship by Decision (7-11)
7-11 What right does Christ have to be Lord over your life?

11 What is involved in surrendering to Christ's lordship?

11 What are the alternatives to making Christ the Lord of your life?

7-11 Do you feel most Christians submit to Christ's lordship? Why or why not?

7-11 What have you done to show your response to Christ's lordship?

_____

_____

_____

_____

Acknowledge His Lordship in Practice (12-19)

13 What does it mean to humble ourselves "under God's mighty hand" (1 Peter 5:6)?

13 What is the connection between being humble and casting all our cares on God?

14 When do you keep cares and worries to yourself?

_____

_____

_____

_____

_____

Summary

In what areas have you experienced growth in submitting to Christ's lordship?

Your "lead-off" question to begin discussion on each section should be a "how" or "why" question, and should be directed to the group as a whole rather than to a particular person.

CHAPTER THREE
FAITH AND THE PROMISES OF GOD

Chapter objective: *To know that our faith should be based on the promises of God in the Bible.*

Good questions for discussion include 4, 9, 10, 13, and 18. Encourage the group to allow plenty of time before your next session for thinking through and completing the chart in question 19 of Chapter 4.

Walking by Faith (Questions 1-5)
  1-2 How does the Bible describe faith?
  3-4 Why is faith the basis of the Christian life?
   5 Why is unbelief a sin?
  1-5 If you are facing a difficult circumstance now, how can you respond to it by faith in God?

_____

_____

_____

_____

Objects of Faith (6-9)
  6-9 Which is more important—the amount of faith we have or the object of our faith? Why?
  6-9 Is faith something we receive from God?

_____

_____

_____

Examples of Faith (10)
  10 How can we follow these examples of faith?

_____

_____

_____

_____

The Promises of God (11-13)

11-13 What is a promise?

_____

_____

_____

_____

_____

Promises to Claim (14-18)

14-18 What does it mean to claim a promise?

14-18 What is one scriptural promise you can claim now?

_____

_____

_____

_____

_____

Summary

What promises from God are you claiming for your life?

Help each group member realize that it is his responsibility both to contribute to and profit from the group discussion.

CHAPTER FOUR
KNOWING GOD'S WILL

Chapter objective: *To learn how to practically seek and know God's will.*

Allow plenty of time for discussing question 19. Other good questions for discussion include 7, 10, and 13.

The Revealed Will of God (Questions 1-5)
    1 How far in advance can we expect God to reveal his will to us?

    1 Why is it essential for us to understand God's will?

    3 What are specific things God wants for every Christian?

_____

_____

_____

_____

_____

Principles of Decision-making (6-17)
    6 How would you explain Matthew 6:33 to a younger Christian?

    6 What is your understanding of a holy life (1 Peter 1:15)?

  11 What does it mean to be conformed to this world?

  12 How does the Holy Spirit guide us?

  14 What qualities would you look for in a counselor?

6-17 How can we know our decisions are based on God's will?

6-17 What is the most important principle in decision-making?

_____

_____

_____

_____

_____

Principles in Practice (18-19)

19 What is the main thing you learned in filling out
this chart?

_____

_____

_____

_____

_____

Aim for simplicity. Make sure the questions you ask are
easily understood. Ask only one question at a time.

CHAPTER FIVE
WALKING AS A SERVANT

Chapter objective: *To follow Christ's example in giving ourselves as servants to others.*

Provide your group with information on how to give financially to various missionaries and missionary organizations. You may also want to organize together a service project to fill a need in your church or community.

Good questions for discussion include 7, 8, 10, and 15.

Christ Your Example (Questions 1-4)
1-4 Why did Jesus become a servant?
2 Why do you think Jesus washed his disciples' feet (John 13:3-5)?

_____

_____

_____

_____

_____

Christ's Desire for You (5-8)
7 Why do you think the disciples were discussing which one of them would be greatest?
7-8 Why did Jesus emphasize servanthood so much?

_____

_____

_____

_____

Giving Yourself (9-10)
9-10 What do you think is the real test of being a servant?
9 How was Paul a servant for Jesus Christ?

_____
_____
_____
_____
_____

Keys to Becoming a Servant (11-16)
13 What is important about listening to others?

_____
_____
_____
_____
_____

A Servant Gives (17-20)
17-20 How is giving related to servanthood?

_____
_____
_____
_____

Summary
What can you give to others in order to truly serve them?

> You can tell by the puzzled faces in the group if one of your questions isn't understood. Restate the question in a different form.

GUIDELINES FOR LEADING DISCUSSIONS

- Don't be afraid of silence after asking a question. Give everyone time to think.
- Remember that the Scriptures are the source of truth. Often you may want to have someone read aloud the verses listed for the study questions as you discuss your answers.
- Summarize frequently. Help the group see the direction of the discussion.
- Your own attitude is a key factor in the group's enthusiasm. Develop a genuine interest in each person's remarks, and expect to learn from them.
- Participate in the discussion as a member of the group. Don't be either a lecturer or a silent observer.
- Close each discussion session in group prayer.

BOOK FOUR

THE CHARACTER OF THE CHRISTIAN

CHAPTER ONE
THE CALL TO FRUITFUL LIVING

Chapter objective: *To understand that living life to the fullest requires holiness in our thoughts, speech, and actions.*

You may want to review the Wheel and Hand illustrations as you begin Book Four. Ask the group members to evaluate their lives by rating themselves on a scale of one to five in each area of these two illustrations. Ask them also to write out ways in which they are experiencing success in some of the areas, and any adjustments they plan to make because of any areas of deficiency.

Good questions for discussion include 1, 5, 19, and 20.

God's Desire for Your Fruitfulness (Questions 1-5)
1-5 Why does God desire us to be fruitful?
1 How would you explain John 15:4-5 to another Christian?
3 What is the relationship between the teachings in John 15:4-5 and Galatians 5:22-23?
3 Which of these qualities do you feel the person on your right most exhibits in his life?

_____

_____

_____

_____

_____

Growing in Character (6-11)
7 How related to each other are the areas mentioned in these three verses?
10 What changes do you want to see in your character?

_____

_____

_____

_____

_____

Godly Wisdom (12-15)

13 How can you know whether you are using godly wisdom or worldly wisdom?

14 How do we receive God's wisdom?

12-15 Can you think of a recent incident in which you showed ungodly wisdom? Why did this happen?

_____

_____

_____

_____

_____

The Joy of Holy Living (16-20)

16-20 What for you is the greatest joy in the Christian life?

16 What does it mean to experience Christ's full joy in our lives?

_____

_____

_____

_____

_____

Summary

In which of these areas—thoughts, speech, or actions— do you feel God wants you now to concentrate most on developing more holiness?

Make a conscious effort to make each group member feel relaxed and part of the group.

43

CHAPTER TWO
GENUINE LOVE IN ACTION

Chapter objective: *To see that love requires a deliberate decision of the will and an attitude of humility.*

Have someone read aloud the quote from 1 Corinthians 13 on page 20.

Good questions for discussion include 3, 8, 12, and 18.

For a project in character growth, suggest that each group member read and pray over a chapter of Proverbs each day for a month as a quiet time exercise. Discuss together week by week the things you are learning from Proverbs.

What Is Genuine Love? (Questions 1-3)
1 What do you think it means that "love never fails" (1 Corinthians 13:8)?

_____

_____

_____

_____

_____

The Direction of Your Love (4-6)
6 What is the relationship between knowing about real love and showing it?

6 Does God limit his love to anyone? Explain your answer.

_____

_____

_____

_____

_____

Love in Humility (7-12)
7 Is there ever a proper time to have pride in your wisdom, strength, or riches (Jeremiah 9:23-24)? Explain.

44

_____

_____

_____

_____

_____

Love in Speech (13-15)
13-15 Why is speech so important in regard to love?

_____

_____

_____

_____

_____

Love in Good Works (16-19)
16 What are some good works you can think of?

_____

_____

_____

_____

_____

Summary
What deliberate decisions of the will should you make in order to show love to others in your life?

> Make an effort to meet at least occasionally with the group members outside your regular discussion session. Use the time to help them individually in their Christian growth, and to discuss their concerns and questions.

CHAPTER THREE
PURITY OF LIFE

Chapter objective: *To recognize the importance of God's moral absolutes in our relationships with others, and to depend on the Scriptures as our authority for moral living.*

Suggest Jerry White's *Honesty, Morality, and Conscience* (NavPress) as outside reading.

Good questions for discussion include 8, 15, 16, and 20.

God's Standard (Questions 1-4)
    2 How can we have a pure heart?
    3 How can we meet these standards realistically?

_____

_____

_____

_____

_____

_____

The Importance of Personal Purity (5-8)
  5-8 What effect does impurity have on your relationship to God?
    5 Why is immorality wrong?
    8 Which of these excuses do you think are most common?

_____

_____

_____

_____

_____

_____

The Path to Purity (9-13)
  9-13 What is the first step on the path to purity?
   12 What does it mean to clothe ourselves with the Lord Jesus (Romans 13:14)?

_____

_____

_____

_____

_____

Personal Relationships (14-15)

15 Why should we set personal standards in our relationships with the opposite sex?

_____

_____

_____

_____

Perspective on Marriage (16-20)

16 What does it mean in God's eyes for a man and a woman to be married?

_____

_____

_____

_____

Summary

Why should the Scriptures be the moral standard for your life?

> A good way to close each session is to summarize what has been discussed, then motivate the group by sharing with them how important this topic is, and finally close in group prayer.

CHAPTER FOUR
INTEGRITY IN LIVING

Chapter objective: *To practice honesty in every area of our life.*

Suggest reading about the life of Joseph (Genesis 37-50) as an extra project. You can discuss this in your next session. Good questions for discussion include 2, 7, 13, and 18.

The Struggle for Integrity (Questions 1-4)
1-4 Why is it a battle to maintain integrity?
2 Why are our hearts so deceptive?
1-4 What is your biggest struggle in maintaining integrity?

_____

_____

_____

_____

_____

Dishonesty Exposed (5-11)
5 What is our conscience?
6 Why do you think Jesus was so critical of hypocrisy?

_____

_____

_____

_____

_____

The Practice of Honesty (12-13)
13 Is there ever a time when a believer should not submit to an authority? If so, when?

_____

_____

_____

_____

Honesty in Speech (14-19)
    14 Why does speech begin in the heart?
    14-19 How does what you say reveal what you are?

_____

_____

_____

_____

_____

Summary
Why do you believe you should demonstrate honesty in every area of your life?

Remember that unless your group has knowledge to share, the discussion method will not work. Encourage each member to complete his study preparation each week, and keep the discussion time centered on what the Scriptures say and how they can be applied to daily life.

CHAPTER FIVE
CHARACTER IN ACTION

Chapter objective: *To know that God ordains suffering in our lives to help produce godly character in us; and to be thankful in all circumstances.*

Try to differentiate in your discussion between suffering for Christ's sake and suffering as a consequence of our own mistakes and wrongdoing.

Suggested reading: the NavPress booklet *Christlikeness* by Jim White.

Have someone read aloud the poem on page 47.

Good questions for discussion include 4, 9, 13, 19, and 21.

God's Ultimate Control (Questions 1-4)

2 What does this incident reveal about Joseph?

3 What does it mean that in all things God works for our good?

_____

_____

_____

_____

_____

The Purpose of Suffering (5-9)

5-9 Why must Christians suffer?

5-9 What are some of the kinds of suffering we may have to endure?

_____

_____

_____

_____

_____

Your Response to Suffering (10-16)

15 Why are our attitudes in life so important?

16 When suffering, is it ever right to ask God, "Why me?" Explain your answer.

_____

_____

_____

_____

_____

The Results of Suffering (17-21)
17 Why does hope follow suffering, perseverance, and
    character?
18 When does God discipline us?
19 How does God comfort us?

_____

_____

_____

_____

_____

Summary
Are you prepared to accept any degree of suffering which
God allows in your life?

> The skillful use of questions is a crucial factor in the
> success of a group discussion. Plan your questions
> carefully.

WHEN THE DISCUSSION STARTS TO WANDER

At times the group discussion may seem to wander from the topics in the chapter. A good rule to follow is to let the group talk about a topic as long as the members seem to be profiting from the exchange of information, and if the discussion is helpful in gaining an overall understanding of the chapter's subject. But don't allow the discussion to wander aimlessly. Ask a question that will get the group back on track.

BOOK FIVE

FOUNDATIONS FOR FAITH

CHAPTER ONE
WHO IS GOD?

Chapter objective: *To praise and worship God more deeply.*

Suggested reading for Book Five: *The Knowledge of the Holy* (Harper and Row) or *The Pursuit of God* (several publishers), both by A.W. Tozer.
Good questions for discussion include 2, 5, 7, 12, and 18.

What Is God Like? (Questions 1-8)
    1-8 Who does God say he is?
      3 What does it mean to you that God must be worshiped in spirit and truth (John 4:24)?
    1-8 Which of God's attributes do you feel you know the least about?

_____

_____

_____

_____

_____

_____

What Does God Do? (9-12)
    9-12 How does God demonstrate his power?
    11 How is God's love expressed in action?

_____

_____

_____

_____

_____

_____

What Does God Expect from You? (13-18)
    13-18 Why does God desire anything from us?
    14 How does one obtain a broken spirit and a contrite heart?

_____

_____

_____

_____

_____

Summary

What things do you most want to praise God for at this time?

> Don't give the impression that as the leader you do not need help in the areas you are discussing. Use the word _we_ rather than _you_. Say, "How should _we_ apply this passage?"

CHAPTER TWO
THE AUTHORITY OF GOD'S WORD

Chapter objective: *To gain greater appreciation of the Scriptures as the trustworthy word of God.*

Good questions for discussion include 8, 9, 13, 17, and 21.

The Author of the Scriptures (Questions 1-3)
1-3 On what basis does the Bible's authority rest?
1-3 What difference does it make who wrote the Scriptures?

_____

_____

_____

_____

_____

Jesus' View of Scripture (4-9)
4 What can we learn from Jesus' encounter with Satan?

_____

_____

_____

_____

The Reliability of the Scriptures (10-13)
10-13 What does it mean to be reliable?
10-13 How can we know the Scriptures are reliable?

_____

_____

_____

_____

_____

The Sufficiency of the Scriptures (14-17)

14-17   How can the Bible be sufficient for every area of life?

15   What does it mean to sow the word?

_____

_____

_____

_____

_____

Applying the Bible to Your Life (18-21)

18-21   What is the most important way the Bible makes a difference in your life today?

_____

_____

_____

_____

Summary

Why must we apply the Scriptures to our daily living?

After a section has been discussed, summarize the direction your discussion has taken. This reinforces what you have been talking about. Then summarize the entire discussion at the end of your time together.

CHAPTER THREE
THE HOLY SPIRIT

Chapter objective: *To examine how the Holy Spirit is present in each believer, and gives gifts to each one.*

Good questions for discussion include 8, 15, and 16.
Have someone read aloud the information about the Trinity on page 22.
Suggested reading: Billy Graham's *The Holy Spirit* (Word, Inc.).

Who Is the Holy Spirit? (Questions 1-3)
1-3 How would you describe the Holy Spirit?
1-3 How would you explain the Trinity?

_____

_____

_____

_____

Who Has the Holy Spirit? (4-8)
4-8 How does a person acquire the Holy Spirit?
7 What does it mean that you are a temple of God?

_____

_____

_____

_____

The Work of the Holy Spirit (9-12)
9-12 What is the purpose of the Holy Spirit?
11 How does the Holy Spirit help you live in obedience to God?

_____

_____

_____

_____

The Gifts of the Holy Spirit (13-16)

13-16 What are the spiritual gifts you have recognized in other Christians you know?

_____

_____

_____

_____

_____

Your Responsibility (17-21)

20 What do you think it means to "put out the Spirit's fire" (1 Thessalonians 5:19)?

20 What does it mean to "grieve the Holy Spirit" (Ephesians 4:30)?

_____

_____

_____

_____

_____

Summary

What does it mean to be Spirit-filled?

Emphasize to your group that the way of discipleship is not easy. Rather, it is costly. Help them see the cost.

CHAPTER FOUR
SPIRITUAL WARFARE

Chapter objective: *To realize that every Christian is engaged in a spiritual battle with Satan, and that God has given us the means for victory.*

Good questions for discussion include 8, 10, 13, 17, and 19.

The Battle (Questions 1-2)
1-2 What is the battle we are in?

_____

_____

_____

_____

Know Your Enemy (3-8)
3-8 How do you know you have a spiritual enemy?
5 How does Satan try to deceive you?
6 What does it mean that Satan is a murderer (John 8:44)?

_____

_____

_____

_____

_____

The Conflict with Sin (9-14)
9-14 Why do we have such a battle with sin?
12-13 What does the world system have to offer?
14 What is the "crown of life" that God promises to those who love him?

_____

_____

_____

_____

_____

The Assurance of Victory (15-17)
    15 What is the extent of Satan's power?
    15 Why was Christ's death so essential for us?
    17 What is the victory God gives us?

_____

_____

_____

_____

_____

Daily Victory (18-22)
    18-19 What to you are the most important factors for living in day-by-day obedience to the Lord?

_____

_____

_____

_____

_____

Summary
    What weapons are you now using most as you wage spiritual warfare?

In asking questions your goal is not to merely get answers, but to bring about discussion. Avoid questions that require only short, categorical answers.

CHAPTER FIVE
THE RETURN OF CHRIST

Chapter objective: *To grow in our hope for the return of Christ.*

Good questions for discussion include 7, 15, 16, and 18.

The Promise of His Return (Questions 1-4)

1-4 How do you know Jesus Christ will return?

1 What do you think it means that Christ is preparing a place for us?

3 What does it mean that Jesus will come in *glory* (Matthew 16:27 and Mark 13:26)?

_____

_____

_____

_____

_____

_____

_____

Conditions Preceding His Return (5-7)

5-7 How would you summarize what the world will be like just before Jesus comes?

5-7 How do present events indicate that prophecy is being fulfiled?

_____

_____

_____

_____

_____

_____

Events at His Return (8-12)

8-12 Describe these future events in your own words.

8-12 How should your knowledge of these events affect your life now?

_____

_____

_____

_____

_____

What His Return Means to You (13-19)
13-19   What aspect of his coming do you most look for-
        ward to?

_____

_____

_____

_____

_____

Summary
What are you motivated to do by knowing Christ is coming again?

> A competent leader always respects the thoughts,
> opinions, and feelings of the members of his group,
> thus creating a positive atmosphere for discussion.

BOOK SIX

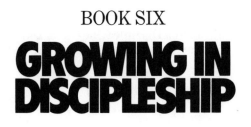

CHAPTER ONE
WHAT IS A DISCIPLE?

Chapter objective: *To examine the commitments required of a disciple of Jesus Christ.*

Good questions for discussion include 1, 3, 4, and 12.
Suggested reading: Lorne Sanny's booklet *Marks of a Disciple* (NavPress).

Jesus' Definition of a Disciple (Questions 1-4)
1 How can you tell if you love anyone else above Christ?

_____

_____

_____

_____

The Disciple Is a Learner (5-9)
5 What are some things you do not like to receive instruction or correction for?
6 From whom do you feel you learn the most?

_____

_____

_____

_____

_____

The Cost of Discipleship (10-14)
10 Why does Christ want us to count the cost of our discipleship?
10-14 Why is there a cost?

_____

_____

_____

_____

_____

Diligence and Discipline (15-22)

16 How can we maintain our eyes on Jesus?

15-22 How can an undisciplined person become more
disciplined?

_____

_____

_____

_____

_____

Summary

What do you feel are your most important commitments
as a disciple of Jesus Christ?

If you allow the discussion to wander aimlessly, it will
soon become boring. Reestablish the purpose and direction of the discussion when you need to.

CHAPTER TWO
THE RESPONSIBLE STEWARD

Chapter objective: *To realize our responsibility to God for the way we use what he has given us.*

Suggested reading: Charles E. Hummel's booklet *Tyranny of the Urgent* (InterVarsity Press).
Good questions for discussion include 4, 7, 8, 12, and 16.

Stewards of God's Resources (Questions 1-3)
2 Can you think of other areas in which you should be a faithful steward?

_____

_____

_____

_____

_____

Use of Time (4-9)
5 What are some characteristics of a successfully managed family?
6 Why is work essential?

_____

_____

_____

_____

Use of Gifts (10-12)
11 How can you get a realistic evaluation of yourself and your spiritual gifts?

_____

_____

_____

_____

Use of Money (13-16)

13-16 What to you are the most important scriptural principles regarding our use of money?

_____

_____

_____

_____

_____

Care of the Body (17-20)

17-20 Why is proper care of the body important?

_____

_____

_____

_____

_____

Summary

In what area do you feel you need most to exercise better stewardship?

Two broad goals for the disciple of Jesus Christ are evangelism and helping other Christians grow as disciples. Evaluate how your group members are doing in these areas, and help them where you can.

CHAPTER THREE
HELPING OTHERS FIND CHRIST

Chapter objective: *To gain more skill in witnessing to others.*

Discuss the idea of having at least some of the group members begin an evangelistic Bible study group in their home with their non-Christian friends. Help them plan and begin this. Challenge your group in this and other ways of sharing the gospel.

Good questions for discussion include 1, 9, 16, 17, and 18.

How to Prepare (Questions 1-4)
2 What do you think it means to truly follow Christ?

_____

_____

_____

_____

_____

Making Contact (5-7)
5 Why do you think Jesus associated with these people?

_____

_____

_____

_____

_____

Recognizing Needs (8-9)
8 How can we follow Jesus' example in recognizing the needs of others?

_____

_____

_____

_____

_____

Using the Scriptures (10-13)

10-13 What are your favorite passages pertaining to the gospel?

_____

_____

_____

_____

_____

Presenting Christ (14-16)

14-16 How can Christ be honored through our verbal witness about him?

_____

_____

_____

_____

Handling Objections (17-18)

17 Why do people bring up objections like these?

_____

_____

_____

_____

Summary

Complete this sentence: My greatest difficulty in sharing Christ with others is . . . .

Work at combining the contributions of individual group members to show that together you can find needed answers and solve common problems.

CHAPTER FOUR
FOLLOW-UP

Chapter objective: *To look at the importance and the practical aspects of helping a young Christian grow into spiritual maturity.*

Good questions for discussion include 5, 6, 14, and 18.

What is Follow-up? (Question 1)
1 What are the most important things you have to share with younger Christians?

_____

_____

_____

_____

_____

Why Follow-up? (2-4)
2-4 What have been the major needs in your own life for growing spiritually?

_____

_____

_____

_____

_____

The Worth of Each Individual (5-9)
5-9 How does this topic relate to helping younger Christians grow?

_____

_____

_____

_____

_____

_____

Helping Others Grow (10-14)

11 Why is prayer important in helping someone else grow spiritually?

_____

_____

_____

_____

_____

Being an Example (15-19)

15-19 Who in your life has provided the best example to help you grow spiritually?

_____

_____

_____

_____

_____

Summary

Do you believe God wants to use you to help others grow in their Christian life? Why or why not?

The price of excellence is careful planning. Take the time you need to prepare adequately for each discussion session. This preparation includes prayer.

CHAPTER FIVE
WORLD VISION

Chapter objective: *To try to see the world from God's point of view.*

Have someone read aloud the information on page 43 under the heading "Some Practical Ways to Look on the Field."

Good questions for discussion include 5, 7, 11, 13, and 14.

God's Concern for the World (Questions 1-4)
1-4 What things have already developed your world vision?

_____

_____

_____

_____

_____

The World Today (5-8)
8 Why do you think there are so few workers for the harvest?

_____

_____

_____

_____

_____

Multiplication (9-11)
9-11 How would you explain the principle of multiplication?

_____

_____

_____

_____

How Do You Fit In? (12-14)

13 What important things can we pray for that will reflect world vision?

_____

_____

_____

_____

_____

Summary

Do you feel you are better able now to see the world from God's point of view? Why or why not?

> If you are talking as much as half the time during your group discussion, you're talking too much. Don't give the group the idea that you are the source of truth. Truth should be discovered in and shared from the Scriptures. Help all your group members experience this.

BOOK SEVEN

A CHAPTER ANALYSIS STUDY OF 1 THESSALONIANS

1 THESSALONIANS: YOUR SURVEY

Objective: *To learn how to do a book survey by getting an overall view of 1 Thessalonians.*

As you begin Book Seven, many of your group members—and perhaps you as well—are starting chapter analysis Bible study for the first time. This study method is not complex, and it will provide a wealth of enlightenment as you learn to see books of the Bible as a whole.

More so than in the first six books of *Design for Discipleship*, each person's written work will probably vary a good deal from anyone else's in the group. It is important to allow enough discussion time for each one to share his discoveries.

Encourage the group members to take notes in their own books on what others are sharing, especially for questions 6, 8, and 9.

You should devote the largest portion of your time to a discussion of your overviews in question 11.

Personal concern and consideration are the keys to having a loving attitude toward your group members. How much do you care about their spiritual growth? How much do you respect their thoughts and feelings?